100 YEARS OF

Women's

WISDOM

100 YEARS OF

Women's
WISDOM

Timeless Insights from
Great Women of the 20th Century

Compiled and Edited by
Angela Beasley Freeman

WALNUT GROVE PRESS
Nashville, TN 37211

ISBN 1-58334-003-3

The ideas expressed in this book are not, in all cases, exact quotations, as some have been edited for clarity and brevity. In all cases, the author has attempted to maintain the speaker's original intent. In some cases, material for this book was obtained from secondary sources, primarily print media. While every effort was made to ensure the accuracy of these sources, the accuracy cannot be guaranteed. For additions, deletions, corrections or clarifications in future editions of this text, please write WALNUT GROVE PRESS.

Printed in the United States of America
Cover Design & Page Layout by Bart Dawson
2 3 4 5 6 7 8 9 10 •   01 02 03 04

ACKNOWLEDGMENTS
The author gratefully acknowledges the support of Dick and Mary Freeman and gives special thanks to the Chicago Public Library.

For my teachers in lifetime love:
Claudette & Carlisle Beasley
Angie & Sam Knight
and Criswell Freeman

TABLE OF CONTENTS

INTRODUCTION

We enter the third millennium A.D. with an extraordinary opportunity to look forward with hope and look backward with appreciation. Alongside our dreams for the future are the paths of our past. The new millennium presents infinite possibilities, while the past hundred years have provided a transitional century that sent man to the moon and woman to the boardroom.

When women decided to speak up and stand out in the 1900's, they earned more rights and responsibilities than ever in history. Today, a woman can serve a country as well as a meal and preach a sermon as well as kneel. Virtually every door in the 21st century opens to the sound of a female voice.

This book honors the women whose ideas and inventions merged hearth with heart to find freedom for females everywhere.

Taking Chances

Women in the 20th century launched a movement so forceful that its impact will be felt well into the new millennium. By accepting the challenge to change, courageous women took their chances and made astounding advances. Around the globe, women were willing to wager, and they won.

The women who marched on and moved up can motivate us all. If you are considering a major move, read on. The winning wisdom in this chapter will improve your chances, whatever chances you choose to take.

Take your chances doing things that
may look crazy to other people.

Oprah Winfrey

Until you're ready to look foolish,
you'll never have the possibility
of being great.

Cher

Everybody must learn this lesson
somewhere — that it costs something
to be what you are.

Shirley Abbott

To gain that which is
worth having, it may
be necessary to
lose everything.

Bernadette Devlin

It is more important to live the life one wishes to live, and to go down with it if necessary, quite contentedly, than live more profitably but less happily.

Marjorie Kinnan Rawlings

The achievement matches the risk.

Doris Betts

Mountain-moving faith is not just dreaming and desiring. It is daring to risk failure.

Mary Kay Ash

We can dream, fail and still survive.

Maya Angelou

Real courage is when you know
you're licked before you begin,
but you begin anyway.

Harper Lee

The human soul has need of security
and also of risk.

Simone Weil

Go in over your head, not just
up to your neck.

Dorothea Lange

If you're too careful, you're so occupied with
being careful that you're sure to
stumble over something.

Gertrude Stein

19

*S*ecurity is a superstition,
it does not exist in nature.
Avoiding danger is no safer
in the long run than
outright exposure.

Helen Keller

In successfully surmounting trials, you
develop a powerful, resourceful self-image.

Marsha Sinetar

What is very difficult at first, if we keep on
trying, gradually becomes easier.

Helen Keller

A spirit of fortitude triumphs over
a sense of futility.

Ellen Glasgow

One painful duty fulfilled makes the next
one plainer and easier.

Helen Keller

A faith, confidence and determination
inside your heart will not fail you.

Mary McLeod Bethune

Everyone has talent. What is rare is the courage to follow that talent wherever it leads.

Erica Jong

I am grateful that my one talent, flying, was useful to my country.

Cornelia Clark Fort
First female pilot killed on active duty during World War II

Defeat in this world is no disgrace, if you really fought for the right thing.

Katherine Anne Porter

Talent cannot be exterminated by uncordiality.

Marianne Moore

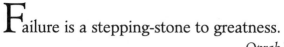
Failure is a stepping-stone to greatness.

Oprah Winfrey

Failure is impossible.

Susan B. Anthony

Mistakes are a fact of life. It's the
response to error that counts.

Nikki Giovanni

Wisdom means not making the
same mistakes over and over again.

Jessica Tandy

Mistakes are usually based in fear.

Suzanne Somers

The thing to do is grab the broom
and drive off the beast of fear.

Zora Neale Hurston

Your goal is not to eliminate fear
but to harness it.

Barbara Braham

The thing you fear most has no power.
Your fear of it is what has the power.
Facing the truth really will set you free.

Oprah Winfrey

By conquering our fears one by one and by
learning to stand up for ourselves and
make decisions, we learn that we
can count on ourselves.

Marsha Sinetar

Believe in yourself; learn and never
stop wanting to build a better world.

Mary McLeod Bethune

Don't ever mind being called tough. Be
strong and have definite ideas and opinions.

Rosalynn Carter

Nothing's ever beaten —
not even eggs in a cake.

Mary Johnston

*Y*ou can't keep a
good woman down.

Alice Walker

MISSION

The 1900's proved that when people pursue their passions, the impossible becomes possible. In 1986, Christa McAuliffe's destiny became history as she boarded the U. S. space shuttle *Challenger*. Before the tragic explosion that took this teacher's life, she said "What are we doing here? We're reaching for the stars."

When you shoot for the stars, you sometimes come up short; yet, as Coretta Scott King reminds us, "If you have nothing worth dying for, you're not really living." Like King and McAuliffe, we all have our dreams. To build your dreams into a true-life mission, follow these instructions...

The future belongs to those who believe in
the beauty of their dreams.

Eleanor Roosevelt

To believe in something not yet proved and
underwrite it with our lives is the way
that we leave the future open.

Lillian Smith

Most people know what they really want
to do. Your purpose will come to you through
your intuition. Every person is intuitive. Many
people, however, don't listen.

Barbara Braham

Try to hear the vague directions whispered
in your ears, and find the road it seems
you must follow.

Zora Neale Hurston

To choose a path with heart, learn how to follow the inner beat of intuitive feeling. Logic may tell where a path may lead but cannot judge whether your heart will be there.

Jean Shinoda Bolen

As we do what we were born to do — as
we love the things we're required to do —
we stimulate a qualitatively superior
energy within ourselves.

Marsha Sinetar

We are not really masters of our fate; except
there may be one powerfully motivating
force that carries us along.

Katherine Anne Porter

To be true to yourself take some action —
no matter how small.

Barbara Braham

All of us can take steps — no matter how
small and insignificant at the start — in
the direction we want to go.

Marsha Sinetar

$\mathscr{T}$o find and fulfill your purpose, you will be called to let go of where you are and go beyond.

Barbara Braham

Be good at "letting go."

Marsha Sinetar

You learn by going where you have to go.

Mia Farrow

Choose a road and stick to it.

Katharine Hepburn

It doesn't matter if it takes a long time getting there; the point is to have a destination.

Eudora Welty

If we forget our past, we won't remember our future, because we won't have one.

Flannery O'Connor

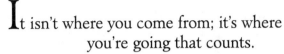
It isn't where you come from; it's where
you're going that counts.

Ella Fitzgerald

Where you come from is not where
you have to stay.

Suzanne Somers

No man can know where he's going,
unless he knows exactly where he's been.

Maya Angelou

We start from our conclusions.

Angela Carter

It's folly to hitch one's wagon to a star
with a harness that doesn't belong to it.

Helen Keller

We must change in order to survive.

Pearl Bailey

If we don't change, we don't grow.
If we don't grow, we are not really living.

Gail Sheehy

You can't change other people, only yourself.

Oprah Winfrey

The first problem for all of us, men and women, is not to learn — but to unlearn.

Gloria Steinem

Only in growth, reform and change, paradoxically enough, is true security found.

Anne Morrow Lindbergh

You've got to continue to grow, or you're just like last night's cornbread — stale and dry.

Loretta Lynn

Whatever has crowded out growth needs to be recognized and removed.

Jean Shinoda Bolen

A woman scandalous perhaps but independent reversed the roles.

Zora Neale Hurston

We aren't what we ought to be. We aren't what we're going to be. We aren't what we want to be. But, thank God, we aren't what we were.

Anonymous

Role reversals are enlightening.

Gloria Steinem

Two things everybody's got to do for
themselves: They've got to trust God, and
they've got to find out about
living for themselves.

Zora Neale Hurston

I have to learn to be myself again....That's all.

Doris Lessing

The only person I'm really
competing with is myself.

Wilma Rudolph
U.S. Olympic Gold Medalist

Life is simple: There's no competition.
There's no race to win.

Suzanne Somers

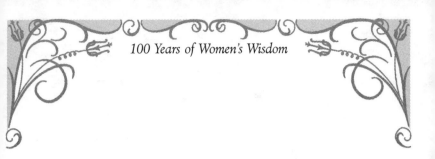

The Miami paper
said she died poor.
But she died rich:
She did something.

Zora Neale Hurston's eulogy

*S*ay yes to destiny.

Jean Shinoda Bolen

3

IN LOVE

The magic of love is a mystery. Playwright Lillian Hellman shares insight when writing, "I don't want to be wise, ever, Mama, ever. I'm in love." In every age, women have heard the raging battle cries of head and heart.

After a heartache or two, it might be tempting to never be tempted again. But, as Iris Murdoch reminds us, "We can only learn to love by loving." Try using this heartwarming advice to warm your heart — or someone else's!

The more I wonder, the more I love.

Alice Walker

There is only one final dignity — love.

Helen Hayes

Love forgets dignity.

Talmud

Love connects us to others.

Jean Shinoda Bolen

Love liberates everything....

Maya Angelou

Nothing compares with being in love.

Oprah Winfrey

A woman who loves always has success.

Vicki Baum

It is not how much we give
but how much love we put in.

Mother Teresa

The most important thing in any relationship
is not what you get but what you give.

Eleanor Roosevelt

The hunger for love is more difficult to feed
than the hunger for bread.

Mother Teresa

Nobody wants to kiss when she's hungry.

Dorothy Dix

Mr. Right is coming; only he must be
in Africa and is walking.

Oprah Winfrey

I tell everybody to travel and not
get married too soon.

Moms Mabley

Love seems to be the unknown country
from which no traveler ever returns.

Zora Neale Hurston

There is a net of love by which
you can catch souls.

Mother Teresa

If grass can grow through cement,
love can find you anywhere.

Cher

Love is like playing checkers.
　　You have to know which man to move.

Moms Mabley

Marriage needs communication —
　　　　and separate baths.

Bette Davis

True marriage — that noble union by
which a man and woman become
together one perfect being.

Florence Nightingale

Grow together as full partners.

Rosalynn Carter

Trust in each other's love.

Kate Chopin

If one is sensible, one never allows oneself
an envious emotion.

Doris Lessing

44

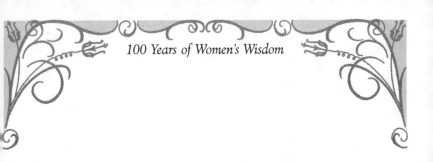

A woman's got to love a
bad man once or twice
in her life to be
thankful for a good one.

Marjorie Kinnan Rawlings

To get to the healing, you have to
break your heart first.

Dorothy Allison

Sometimes your heart will ache.

Ma Rainey

The heart has not stopped.

Sylvia Plath

It never will thump again.

Katherine Mansfield

What really breaks a heart is
taking away its dream.

Pearl Buck

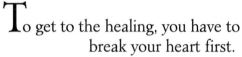

A broken heart is what
makes life so wonderful —
five years later.

Phyllis Battelle

Give me a dozen such heartbreaks, if it
would help me lose a few pounds.

Colette

Great loves, too, must be endured.

Coco Chanel

The heart outgrows old grief.

Ella Wheeler-Wilcox

Your soul tells you when it's time to move on.

Oprah Winfrey

Love that has not friendship for its base is
like a mansion built upon the sand.

Ella Wheeler-Wilcox

Love builds for eternity.

Mary McLeod Bethune

*L*ove lights more fires
than hate can extinguish.

Ella Wheeler-Wilcox

*N*ever think
you've seen the last
of anything.

Eudora Welty

WITH FRIENDS

Often, friends are our most astute advisors. Toni Morrison explains, "A friend gathers all the pieces and gives them back in the right order." Every woman knows the value of having a trusted friend who will lend an ear and give a hand. Such friends are able to talk things through and turn troubles into triumphs.

Hellen Keller notes, "As long as we sweeten another's pain, our lives are not in vain." Truly, our pleasure in living is greatest when giving.

*T*alk is a refuge.

Zora Neale Hurston

The great privilege, relief and comfort
of friendship is that one has
to explain nothing.

Katherine Mansfield

Constant use will not wear ragged
the fabric of friendship.

Dorothy Parker

Friendships, like geraniums,
bloom in kitchens.

Blanche Gelfant

The most called upon requisite of a friend
is an accessible ear.

Maya Angelou

Really intimate conversation is only possible
between two or three people.

Simone Weil

*I*f you listen to
your conscience,
it will serve you as
no other friend
you'll ever know.

Loretta Young

The kindest way of helping yourself
is to find a friend.

Ann Kaiser Stearns

The best time to make friends is
before you need them.

Ethel Barrymore

Friendship with oneself is all-important,
because without it one cannot be friends with
anyone else in the world.

Eleanor Roosevelt

A foreigner is a friend I've yet to meet.

Pearl Buck

Trust in the power of other people who can
help you to accept and love yourself.

Ann Kaiser Stearns

If your experiences would benefit
        anybody, give them to someone.

Florence Nightingale

Advice is what we ask for when
        we already know the answer
        but wish we didn't.

Erica Jong

Please give me some good advice in your
        next letter — I promise not to take it.

Edna St. Vincent Millay

$\mathscr{I}$am very handy with my advice, and then when anybody appears to be following it, I get frantic.

Flannery O'Connor

*O*ld friends are best
unless you catch
a new one fit to make
an old one out of.

Sarah Orne Jewett

She always kept things secret in
such a public way.

Katherine Anne Porter

Keep the other person's well-being in mind
when you feel an attack of soul-purging
truth coming on.

Betty White

When you find yourself judging someone,
silently say to yourself, "They are doing the
best they can right now." Then mentally
forgive yourself for judging.

Marsha Sinetar

My friends have always given me that
supreme proof of devotion: a spontaneous
aversion to the man I love.

Colette

*K*ind words can be
short and easy to speak,
but their echoes are
truly endless.

Mother Teresa

AT HOME

Jane Ace quips, "Home wasn't built in a day," and anyone who's moved recently will agree. Establishing a home of your own takes time, but the energy invested pays a tidy sum.

Whether you live alone, with friends, with children, family, dogs or cats...in hotels, dormitories, or corporate housing...home is your own special place for relaxing, for letting in friends and letting down guards. This chapter unlocks the secret to a welcome home.

My only concern was to get home
after a hard day's work.

Rosa Parks

The serving of good food is one certain way
of pleasing everybody.

Marjorie Kinnan Rawlings

You waste good life when
you waste good food.

Katherine Anne Porter

My kitchen is a mystical place,
a kind of temple.

Pearl Bailey

Too many cooks may spoil the broth,
but it only takes one to burn it.

Julia Child

Neither knowledge nor diligence can
create a great chef.

Colette

It takes more than ingredients to cook a good
meal. The cook must put in some
enjoyment and spontaneity.

Pearl Bailey

Cleaning your house while your kids are still
growing up is like shovelling the walk
before it stops snowing.

Phyllis Diller

When you live alone, you can be sure the
person who squeezed the toothpaste tube in
the middle wasn't committing a hostile act.

Ellen Goodman

Until now, I've been vice president in charge
of dusting. Now, I'll have to sweep up, too.

Lucille Ball

If it won't catch fire today, clean it tomorrow.

Erma Bombeck

"Excuse my dust."

epitaph Dorothy Parker chose for herself

One of the oldest human needs is having someone to wonder where you are when you don't come home at night.

Margaret Mead

Where, after all, do universal human rights begin? In small places, close to home.

Eleanor Roosevelt

The quality of your life is measured by the little things.

Barbara Braham

What can you do
to promote world peace?
Go home and
love your family.

Mother Teresa

upon receiving the Nobel Peace Prize

The average family only exists on paper, and its average budget is fiction.

Sylvia Porter

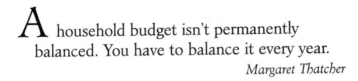

A household budget isn't permanently balanced. You have to balance it every year.

Margaret Thatcher

One of the luckiest things that can happen to you in life is to have a happy childhood.

Agatha Christie

Remember childhood visions.

Mary McLeod Bethune

Don't let a bad childhood stand in your way.

Oprah Winfrey

We want far better reasons to have children than not knowing how to prevent them.

Dora Russell

In general, my children refuse to eat
anything that hasn't danced on television.

Erma Bombeck

Children must invent their own games
and teach the old ones how to play.

Nikki Giovanni

Never help a child with a task at which
he feels he can succeed.

Maria Montessori

It's very important you give children a chance.

Nikki Giovanni

Give curiosity freedom.

Eudora Welty

*A*ny mother could
perform the jobs of several
air-traffic controllers
with great ease.

Lisa Alther

The doctors told me
I would never walk,
but my mother told me
I would — so
I believed my mother.

Wilma Rudolph

U.S. Olympic Gold Medalist

Mothers are really the
true spiritual teachers.

Oprah Winfrey

When Mama talks, listen;
it's the truth she's telling.

Dorothy Allison

Mother's room and mother's need for
privacy become a valuable lesson in
respect for other people's rights.

Doris Lessing

A woman must have money
and a room of her own....

Virginia Woolf

Some sort of silent trade takes place between mothers and children.

YuOko Tsushima

Tears suddenly come to a mother's eyes when she watches her child be happy!

Elizabeth Jolley

Laughter and crying are twin expressions.

Ai Bei

There's a connection between
pain and pleasure.

Phyllis Diller

With each celebration of maturity,
there is a pang of loss.

Louise Erdich

Childhood is short;
regret nothing of the hard work.

Doris Lessing

Treat the world well. It was not given to you
by your parents but lent to you
by your children.

Ida B. Wells

The job of parents is to guide, not to own.
Our children are not ours.

Suzanne Somers

In the end, it's not what you do for your
children but what you've taught them
to do for themselves.

Ann Landers

Our human problem — one common to
parents, sons and daughters — is letting go
while holding tight to the unraveling
yarn that ties our hearts.

Louise Erdich

*N*ow go and seek
your fortune, Darling.

Angela Carter

AT WORK

The 1900's made all the world a stage for women, as females began earning international acclaim by playing major roles. From presidents of countries to owners of companies, women began choosing careers that were no longer behind the scenes.

In her book *Do What You Love and the Money Will Follow*, Marsha Sinetar writes, "Any work can provide your life with so much enjoyment that it begins to be experienced as 'play.'" If you'd like to turn your workshop into a playground, build on the ideas that follow.

To love what you do and feel that
it matters — how could anything be more fun?

Katherine Graham

Work is the nearest thing to happiness
that I can find.

Zora Neale Hurston

Our Girl Scouting rules: Play fair. Play for
your side and not for yourself. And, as for
the score, the best thing in a game
is the fun — not the result.

Juliette Low

Playing is a vital part of life.

Dinah Shore

*L*ove only what you do
and not what
you have done.

Adrienne Rich

It's not the matter of the work but the mind
that goes into it which counts.

Ellen Glasgow

Whether you think you can or think
you can't — you're right.

Mary Kay Ash

When young people ask me how I made it,
I say, "It's absolutely hard work. Nobody's
gonna' wave a magic wand."

Loretta Lynn

What the world really needs is
more love and less paperwork.

Pearl Bailey

To work, even in poverty and obscurity,
is worthwhile.

Virginia Woolf

Success isn't everything,
but it makes you
stand straight.

Lillian Hellman

*S*ometimes I feel like
a cat among tigers.

Katherine Mansfield

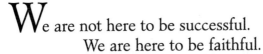
We are not here to be successful.
We are here to be faithful.

Mother Teresa

The motivation of a "workaholic"
is usually fear.

Marsha Sinetar

Never lose your zeal for building
a better world.

Mary McLeod Bethune

If you can't do it with feeling, don't.

Patsy Cline

Knowing what you cannot do is more
important than knowing what you can do.

Lucille Ball

People who fight fire with fire usually
end up with ashes.

Abigail Van Buren

Always try to be smarter than
the people who hire you.

Lena Horne

There are two kinds of talent: God-given and
man-made. With man-made talent, you have
to work very hard. With God-given talent,
you just touch it up once in a while.

Pearl Bailey

Any talent we are born with
eventually surfaces.

Marsha Sinetar

It's regrettable when manners
are subordinate to matter.

Marianne Moore

Good manners will often
take people where
neither money nor
education will take them.

Fanny Jackson Coppin

The best way to run a business is the way
you run your life.

Oprah Winfrey

Doing your best at this moment puts you in
the best place for the next moment.

Oprah Winfrey

Excellence costs a great deal.

May Sarton

Ideas are a dime a dozen. People who
implement them are priceless.

Mary Kay Ash

A mediocre idea that generates enthusiasm
will go further than a great idea
that inspires no one.

Mary Kay Ash

The speed of the leader is
the speed of the gang.

Mary Kay Ash

Discipline is a powerful tool for getting
what you want out of life.

Marsha Sinetar

List your goals. Then list ten to twenty
activities to help reach the goal. A goal
is not "do-able," but an activity is.

Marsha Sinetar

Goal attainment can feel shallow since
it's the *process* of accomplishment
that gives life meaning.

Barbara Braham

You can't do it all yourself. Don't be afraid to
rely on others to help you accomplish your goals.

Oprah Winfrey

At work, you think of the children you've left at home. At home, you think of the work you've left unfinished.

Golda Meir

I have never felt the fact of being a woman
put me at a disadvantage.

Katherine Anne Porter

I think like a man. I just look like a woman.

Dolly Parton

The best compliment a man can pay
a woman is to tell her that...
she thinks like a woman.

Margaret Thatcher

I have made enough money to support myself,
and I'm not afraid of being alone.

Katharine Hepburn

I earn and pay my own way,
as a great many women do today.

Dinah Shore

One of the largest enemies we need to
deal with is our own expectations
and attitudes toward money.

Marsha Sinetar

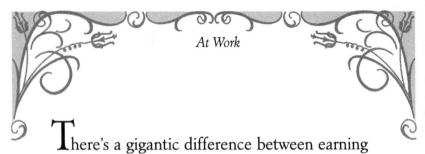

There's a gigantic difference between earning
a great deal of money and being rich.

Marlene Dietrich

The lure of quantity is the most
dangerous of all.

Simone Weil

I find the rich much poorer sometimes;
they're often lonelier inside.

Mother Teresa

No one can figure out
your worth but you.

Pearl Bailey

To be content with little is hard;
to be content with much is impossible.

Marie Ebner-Eschenbach

The more you have, the more you're
occupied; the less you have, the
more free you are.

Mother Teresa

If I do well I am blessed, whether any bless
me or not. And if I do ill, I am cursed.

Marianne Moore

God has a plan for all of us, but He
expects us to do our share of the work.

Minnie Pearl

When it's all over,
the Master isn't going
to ask how many
things you owned.

Oprah Winfrey

MOVING ON

The days come and go so quickly, and the years fly by. Next thing you know it's another millennium. When life moves on, must you?

Margaret Atwood says, "Everyone else my age is an adult; I'm merely in disguise." She's not the only one who's not on the clock: Flannery O'Connor notes, "Time goes so fast, you can't tell if you're young or old." For timeless advice on how to stay ageless, move on to the next page.

It's not how old you are
but how you are old.

Marie Dressler

Age is all imagination. Ignore years and
they'll ignore you.

Ella Wheeler-Wilcox

In youth we learn. In age we understand.

Marie Ebner-Eschenbach

You grow up the day you have your first real
laugh at yourself.

Ethel Barrymore

The trick is to live long enough to put your
young bluffs to use.

Alice Walker

When one's lived many years, the past becomes an attic: One goes there hunting some particular thing and finds everything except what one went to find.

Clara Louise Kellogg

Whaen I count over a few of the things lost in one lifetime — the mysterious losses of canisters, bird cages & jewelry — the wonder is I've any clothes on my back and sit surrounded by solid furniture.

Virginia Woolf

Every time I think I'm getting old, something else happens.

Lillian Carter

I used to dread getting older, because I thought I wouldn't be able to do the things I wanted to do. But now that I'm older, I find I don't want to do them.

Nancy Astor

Whatever wrinkles I got,
I enjoyed getting them.

Ava Gardner

Sometimes I would almost rather have people
take away years of my life than
take away a moment.

Pearl Bailey

As soon as you feel too old
to do a thing, do it.

Margaret Deland

Though it sounds absurd, it is true to say that
I felt younger at sixty than I felt at twenty.

Ellen Glasgow

Do not deprive me of my age.
I have earned it.

May Sarton

*H*aving the ability to love
makes a big difference
in staying young.

Dinah Shore

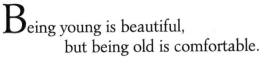

Being young is beautiful,
but being old is comfortable.
Marie Ebner-Eschenbach

After 30, a body has a mind of its own.
Bette Midler

Ah well, perhaps one has to be very old
before one learns how to be amused
rather than shocked.
Pearl Buck

Surely the consolation of old age is finding
out how few things are worth worrying over.
Dorothy Dix

Through the centuries, we faced down death
by daring to hope.

Maya Angelou

I have only one curiosity left: death.

Coco Chanel

Life poses questions and that two-headed
spirit that rules the beginning and end of all
things called Death has all of the answers.

Zora Neale Hurston

The challenge of Death is to be ready
so that you aren't distracted by
unresolved earthly matters.

Lisa Alther

We're all equal in death.

Florence King

98

*L*ife is a party;
you join after it's started,
and you leave
before it's finished.

Elsa Maxwell

*L*ife is just a short walk
from the cradle to grave,
and it sure behooves us
to be kind to one another
along the way.

Alice Childress

GIVING BACK

In 1913, girls in America received a gift that's kept on giving. Juliette Low established the Girl Scouts, thereby proving the power of improving others. For generations, Girl Scouts have trooped through the world with high ideals and sweet ideas.

Low offers this morsel about serving others: "To put yourself in another's place requires real imagination." Try to imagine your own approach to assisting others. And, as a guide to earning your green badge of service, follow these leaders...

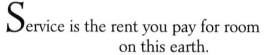
Service is the rent you pay for room
on this earth.

Shirley Chisholm

It's up to each of us to contribute
something to this wonderful world.

Eve Arden

Ultimately, it is through serving others
that we become fully human.

Marsha Sinetar

Nothing makes you like other human
beings so much as doing things for them.

Zora Neale Hurston

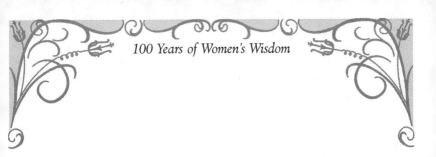

Invest in a human soul.
Who knows? It might be
a diamond in the rough.

Mary McLeod Bethune

A solitary fantasy
can totally transform
a million realities.

Maya Angelou

The woman who is not afraid to use her small means to assist others need not fear poverty.

Ella Wheeler-Wilcox

If you give, do it without boasting.

Lillian Hellman

There are hearts and hands always ready to make generous intentions become noble deeds.

Helen Keller

So it always is. Someone is ever ready to scatter little acts of kindness along our pathway, making it smooth and pleasant.

Helen Keller

Try to make people you know happy.

Alice Walker

It is important to know that life is vital, and one's own living a torn fragment of the larger cloth.

Marjorie Kinnan Rawlings

You enhance other people's lives as you enhance your own.

Marsha Sinetar

When it comes to human desires and
human hopes, we are all the same.

Oprah Winfrey

Love always finds its way to an imprisoned
soul and leads it out into the world
of freedom and intelligence.

Helen Keller

We are defined by the way we treat ourselves
and the way we treat other people.

Oprah Winfrey

Good manners are more like emotions.
One must feel them not merely exhibit them.

Amy Vanderbilt

Words are the most subtle symbols we have,
and our human fabric depends on them.

Iris Murdoch

Writing is a labor of love — a way to
light a candle in a gale wind.

Alice Childress

Paper has more patience than people do.

Anne Frank

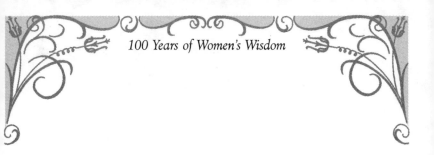
Two kinds of people
on earth can be seen:
The people who lift
and the people who lean.

Ella Wheeler-Wilcox

*E*ncourage people to empower themselves.

Oprah Winfrey

We have to teach as well as learn.

Gloria Steinem

Love is knowing someone — neither as an angel nor animal — but as a human being.

Iris Murdoch

True patriotism is the service of all to all.

Helen Keller

Believe that your tender, loving thoughts and wishes for good have the power to help the struggling souls of earth rise higher.

Ella Wheeler Wilcox

There are no errors
In the great Eternal plan;
And all things work together;
For the final good of man.

Ella Wheeler-Wilcox

9

FINDING STRENGTH

That each sorrow has its purpose
Though the sorrow oft' unguessed,
As sure as the sun brings morning,
Whatever is — is best.
Ella Wheeler-Wilcox

Wheeler-Wilcox, a prolific poet of the 1900's, encourages us to be more receptive to unwelcome sorrow. Why? Because sadness is often short-lived, but its lessons last a lifetime. For a good dose of soul-strengthening pain relief, read on.

'Tis easy enough to be pleasant
    When life flows along like a song,
    But the one worthwhile
        is the one who will smile,
    When everything goes dead wrong.

Ella Wheeler-Wilcox

When we see problems as opportunities for growth, we tap a source of knowledge within ourselves which carries us through.

Marsha Sinetar

There are no mistakes. Everything in life has a purpose. All events are blessings for us to learn from.

Elisabeth Kübler-Ross

The fire that seems so cruel is the light that shows your strength.

Ella Wheeler-Wilcox

*I*can't think of any
sorrow in the world
that a hot bath
wouldn't help.

Susan Glaspell

Don't sidestep suffering; you have to go
through it to get where you're going.

Katherine Anne Porter

It is human misery and not pleasure which
contains the secret of divine wisdom.

Simone Weil

Nothing is really bad; all of life's experiences
are lessons from which to grow.

Suzanne Somers

If you want the rainbow, you've got
to put up with a little rain.

Dolly Parton

If you're unhappy with anything — whatever
is bringing you down — get rid of it.

Tina Turner

*I*t's not the load
that breaks you down;
it's the way you carry it.

Lena Horne

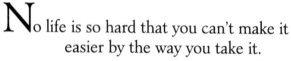
No life is so hard that you can't make it
easier by the way you take it.

Ellen Glasgow

No path is wholly rough.

Ella Wheeler-Wilcox

Be grateful for all of life's experiences,
good and bad.

Suzanne Somers

Facing our losses is part of how we
find our freedom again.

Ann Kaiser Stearns

Sometimes, when you beat your head against
a wall, your heart takes the punishment.

Dinah Shore

A woman is like a tea bag. You never know
how strong she is until she gets into hot water.

Eleanor Roosevelt

Suffering is a by-product of new growth and
is not, in any sense, an end in itself.

Iris Murdoch

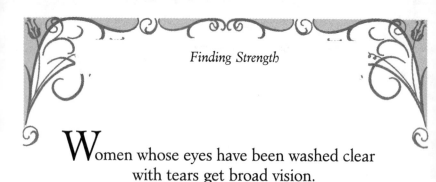

Women whose eyes have been washed clear
with tears get broad vision.

Dorothy Dix

Those who don't know how to weep with their
whole heart don't know how to laugh either.

Golda Meir

Find something to laugh about.

Maya Angelou

The trick is not how much pain you feel
but how much joy you feel.

Erica Jong

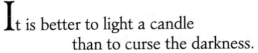

It is better to light a candle
than to curse the darkness.

Eleanor Roosevelt

The excursion is the same when you go
looking for sorrow as when you go
looking for joy.

Eudora Welty

The greatest thing I was ever able to do was
to give a welfare check back saying,
"Here, I don't need this anymore."

Whoopi Goldberg

Sometimes it takes years to really grasp
what's happened in your life.

Wilma Rudolph

Nothing is pointless and nothing is meaning-less. By waiting to know the consequences, we see what an event really was trying to teach us.

Katherine Anne Porter

All events have a purpose. The job in life is
to understand the meaning.

Suzanne Somers

Keep your face to the sunshine
and you cannot see the shadows.

Helen Keller

It would be ungracious to grumble.

Mary Cassat

In a moment everything is altered. The brooding self disappears and, when thinking of the same matter, it now seems less important.

Iris Murdoch

*T*here is nothing
we cannot
live down, rise above
and overcome.

Ella Wheeler-Wilcox

*W*hat becomes of lost opportunities? Perhaps our guardian angel gathers them up and will give them back when we've grown wiser — and will use them rightly.

Helen Keller

10

KEEPING FAITH

Dr. Elisabeth Kübler-Ross earned a degree in medicine to heal bodies — and found herself helping souls, as well. With compassion and competence, Kübler-Ross reminded us of our vital connection between mind, body and soul. Through her extraordinary writings, Dr. Kübler-Ross taught the essential facts of life — and death.

Life's best internal medicine — love — is a proven prescription. If you want to feel your best — both inside and out — mix a healthy dose of faith with a lifetime of love. For some trusted formulas, consider the following.

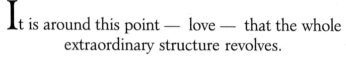

It is around this point — love — that the whole
extraordinary structure revolves.

Doris Lessing

The ultimate lesson we all have to learn
is unconditional love.

Elisabeth Kübler-Ross

Things seen are temporal:
Things unseen are eternal.

Helen Keller

The spiritual life is the most important.

Oprah Winfrey

There are no atheists
on turbulent airplanes.

Erica Jong

I never really look for things. I accept what-ever God throws my way. Whichever way God turns my feet, I go.

Pearl Bailey

Faith can put a candle in the darkest night.

Margaret Sangster

Unreasonable hope is always latent. Perhaps one should open the door to it more often.

Iris Origo

Leave the door open for hope.

Elisabeth Kübler-Ross

Have faith in God, faith in yourself, and
a desire to serve.

Mary McLeod Bethune

Trust in Allah, but tie your camel.

Islamic saying

God can make you anything you want to be,
but you have to put yourself in His hands.

Mahalia Jackson

The only way you can be happy is to determine
what you believe is right and behave in a way
that is consistent with that belief.

Barbara Braham

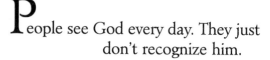

People see God every day. They just
don't recognize him.

Pearl Bailey

If you seek what is honorable, what is truth,
all the other things come as a matter of course.

Oprah Winfrey

The gift of knowing is only useful
if it is shared.

Suzanne Somers

Surround yourself with people you trust.

Oprah Winfrey

*Forgiveness is a gift
you give yourself.*

Suzanne Somers

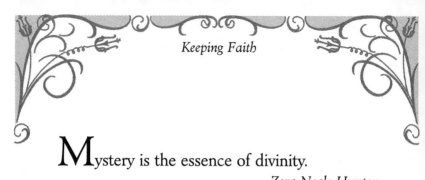

Mystery is the essence of divinity.

Zora Neale Hurston

The laws of the universe are never repealed
to accommodate our follies.

Frances Watkins Harper

Make peace with the universe and
bow to its laws.

Zora Neale Hurston

Messages come to us all the time.
We are all connected this way.

Suzanne Somers

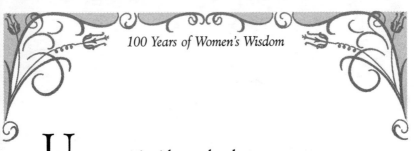

Uncanny coincidence leads to awareness
of an underlying connecting principle.

Jean Shinoda Bolen

Miracles are instantaneous; they cannot be
summoned but come of themselves, usually at
unlikely moments and to those who are least
likely to expect them.

Katherine Anne Porter

Meaningful coincidences touch a deep
feeling in the psyche. These synchronistic
events give us a sense that we're
part of a greater whole.

Jean Shinoda Bolen

Any religion that satisfies the individual urge
is valid for that person.

Zora Neale Hurston

One thing that doesn't abide by majority
rule is a person's conscience.

Harper Lee

It is wonderful how much time good people
spend fighting the devil. But, if they would only
expend the same amount of energy loving their
fellow man, the devil would die in
his own tracks of boredom.

Helen Keller

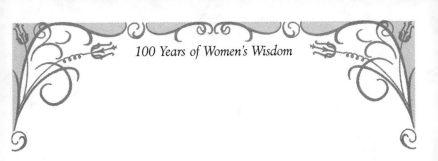

*D*on't cut your
conscience to fit
this year's fashions.

Lillian Hellman

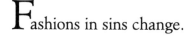

Fashions in sins change.

Lillian Hellman

All sins are attempts to fill voids.

Simone Weil

When you've done a wrong, you have to right that wrong or you can't rest.

Lillian Hellman

Morality is a matter of attention not of will.

Simone Weil

We need a moral philosophy in which the concept of love can once again be made central.

Iris Murdoch

Be honest. Tell the truth. Don't try to think
of something to say; just say
whatever is the truth.

Oprah Winfrey

Speak the truth — no matter what comes of it.

Ellen Glasgow

Happiness is having broad, deep
knowledge — to know true ends from
false and lofty things from low.

Helen Keller

Truth is the goal. Everything seems clearer because it's the truth. By interacting with total honesty, your reward is contentment.

Suzanne Somers

Desire truth. Await it laboriously, distilling words, forever desiring truth.

Virginia Woolf

Ask truth; speak truth; and act truth — now and forever.

Lillian Hellman

Finally, it's honesty that heals.

Suzanne Somers

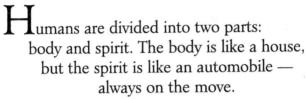

Humans are divided into two parts:
body and spirit. The body is like a house,
but the spirit is like an automobile —
always on the move.

Flannery O'Connor

Life is not linear; it is circular.

Barbara Braham

Dying is the final stage of growth in life.
The self, or spirit — or whatever you wish
to label it — is eternal.

Elisabeth Kübler-Ross

Without faith nothing is possible.
With it, nothing is impossible.

Mary McLeod Bethune

The blessings of this day are enough. It's all any of us can ask.

Lorna Luft

11

WOMEN'S WISDOM

We conclude with some intuitive insight and heartfelt humor from 20th-century women...Enjoy!

*A*ll serious daring
starts from within.

Eudora Welty

There is inside each of us a sixth sense:
a soul sense which sees, hears, and feels
all at the same time.

Helen Keller

When you trust your intuition, you get more
of the truth — and you get it faster
than using your intellect.

Barbara Braham

Learn to get in touch with the silence within
yourself. There's no need to go to India or
somewhere else to find peace. You will
find it in your room, your garden,
or even your bathtub.

Elisabeth Kübler-Ross

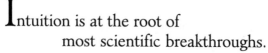

Intuition is at the root of
   most scientific breakthroughs.

Barbara Braham

One needs a capacity for intuiting.

Jean Shinoda Bolen

Intuition cannot be forced.
   Answers need time to incubate.

Barbara Braham

No journey carries one far unless
   it goes an equal distance
   into the world within.

Lillian Smith

Inside is a place where
        springs never dry up.

Pearl Buck

If we go into ourselves, we find that
        we possess exactly what we desire.

Simone Weil

Try not to be afraid of your inwardness.

Ann Kaiser Stearns

If we're willing to take an honest look
        at ourselves, we can grow and mature.

Elisabeth Kübler-Ross

*Y*ou must learn to be still
in the midst of activity
and to be vibrantly
alive in repose.

Indira Gandhi

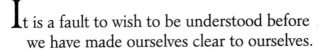

It is a fault to wish to be understood before
we have made ourselves clear to ourselves.

Simone Weil

The hardest thing is learning some things
about ourselves that we don't especially
want to know.

Ann Kaiser Stearns

Self-knowledge is something inward
which shows outwardly.

Iris Murdoch

Self-awareness is probably the most
important thing in becoming a champion.

Billie Jean King

When we swallow a little knowledge of
ourselves, it becomes either
good or sour inside.

Pearl Bailey

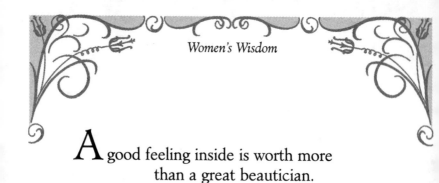

 A good feeling inside is worth more
than a great beautician.

Mother Teresa

 T alk happiness; talk faith; talk health.
Say you are well, or all is well with you,
And God shall hear your words and
make them true.

Ella Wheeler-Wilcox

 I f we change within, our outer life
will change also.

Jean Shinoda Bolen

Once we give up
searching for approval,
we often find
it easier to earn
respect and approval.

Gloria Steinem

*U*ntil you've lost your
reputation, you never
realize what a burden
it was or what
freedom really is.

Margaret Mitchell

The best student is not one who agrees but one who questions.

Doris Betts

A person's intelligence is directly reflected by the number of conflicting attitudes she can bring to bear on the same subject.

Lisa Alther

I cry out for order and find it only in art.

Helen Hayes

Art is not for the cultivated taste — it's to cultivate taste.

Nikki Giovanni

Masterpieces have a strange air of simplicity.

Virginia Woolf

151

Rather than "either/or," life is "and."

Barbara Braham

Live a life full of steady enthusiasm.

Florence Nightingale

Go ahead...be happy as long as you can.

Dorothy Parker

Be kinder to yourself.

Adrienne Rich

Nobody's gonna' live for you.

Dolly Parton

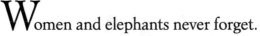

Women and elephants never forget.

Dorothy Parker

Choose to remember the best qualities
of a person, career or experience.

Ann Kaiser Stearns

Being angry with people hurts you
more than them.

Oprah Winfrey

Hold it true that thoughts are things,
Endowed with bodies, breath and wings;
And that we send them forth to fill,
The world with good results or ill.

Ella Wheeler-Wilcox

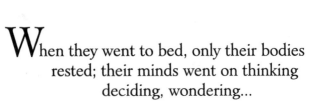

When they went to bed, only their bodies
rested; their minds went on thinking
deciding, wondering...

Katherine Mansfield

The activity of the mind is not so
easily disposed of.

Iris Murdoch

One reason I don't drink is because I want to
know when I'm having a good time.

Nancy Astor

There's no harm in putting a full stop to one's
disagreeable thoughts.

Virginia Woolf

Take the back roads instead of the highways.

Minnie Pearl

The end is nothing. The road is all.

Willa Cather

*D*rive carefully.
The life you save
may be your own.

Flannery O'Connor

If I had it all to do over, I would do it all over again.

Lee Smith

INDEX

Index

If you have enjoyed this book, you will also enjoy the many other inspirational quotation books from WALNUT GROVE PRESS, including *Minutes from the Great Women's Coffee Club* by Angela Beasley.

For more information, please call
1-800-256-8584

For a daily dose of
inspirational wisdom
visit us at
www.quotedoctor.com.